Web 3.0

Unleashing the Power of Decentralized Connectivity

By
Michael McNaught

An educational book for readers of all ages.

Interested in learning about the decentralized web?

Well, this is the book for you!

Copyright

Web 3.0

Unleashing the Power of Decentralized Connectivity

Written By Michael McNaught

Copyright © 2023.

All Rights Reserved.

Preface

-Poem

In the realm of code, where dreams take flight,

Web 3.0 shines with boundless light.

Decentralized and free, it spreads its wings,

A symphony of data, where innovation sings.

Blockchain's embrace, a secure foundation,

Empowering transactions, without hesitation.

Smart contracts reign, with transparency and trust,

A digital revolution, where possibilities combust.

From immersive experiences to AI's embrace,

Web 3.0 unveils a breathtaking space.

Connected worlds and virtual realms unite,

Unleashing the future, with each digital byte.

So let us embark on this wondrous quest,

Where the web evolves, its limits put to rest.

Web 3.0, a beacon of progress and delight,

A testament to human ingenuity's might.

Hi there! My name is Michael McNaught, a scientist by profession, and an avid blockchain and digital currency enthusiast. I enjoy learning about this amazing cutting-edge technology and sharing my knowledge with others.

The internet has come a long way since its inception, revolutionizing the way we communicate, learn, and conduct business. With Web 3.0, a new wave of innovation emerges, characterized by decentralized networks, blockchain technology, and the integration of artificial intelligence. It presents an opportunity to redefine the rules of engagement, to reimagine what is possible, and to shape a digital future that is more equitable, transparent, and inclusive.

Within the pages of this book, we delve into the intricacies of Web 3.0, examining the key technologies, principles, and applications that underpin its foundation. From decentralized finance and digital identity to the Internet of Things and virtual reality, we explore the myriad ways in which Web 3.0 is poised to revolutionize industries, reshape governance structures, and empower individuals in unprecedented ways.

Table of Contents

Chapter 1:

The Evolution of the Web

Section 1: Web 1.0: The Static Web

In the early days of the World Wide Web, its purpose was primarily to deliver static information to users. This era, commonly known as Web 1.0, spanned from the late 1980s to the early 2000s. During this time, websites were limited in their functionality and interactivity, mainly offering one-way communication from the content provider to the user.

Web 1.0 was characterized by the dominance of static HTML pages, where content was created and controlled by a small number of individuals or organizations. Websites were mostly informational in nature, acting as digital brochures or catalogs. Users could access information, browse through text and images, but had limited means to interact with the content or contribute their own.

At that time, websites were primarily built using HTML, a markup language that defined the structure and presentation of web pages. The concept of cascading style sheets (CSS) emerged, allowing developers to separate the presentation from the content. This separation facilitated the standardization of website design and enhanced the user experience by providing consistency across different web pages.

The static nature of Web 1.0 limited the potential for collaboration, social interaction, and dynamic content creation. Websites were essentially static islands of information, lacking the ability to adapt to individual user preferences or respond to real-time changes in the digital landscape. This led to the realization that a new paradigm was necessary to unlock the full potential of the web.

Section 2: Web 2.0: The Rise of User Participation

Web 2.0 marks a significant shift in the evolution of the web, heralding an era of increased user participation, collaboration, and social interaction. This phase emerged in the early 2000s and continues to shape the web we know today.

Unlike its predecessor, Web 2.0 introduced dynamic and interactive features, empowering users to contribute their own content and actively participate in the creation of the web. Social media platforms, blogging sites, and online forums gained prominence, enabling individuals to connect, share information, and engage in discussions. Websites transformed from static repositories of information into vibrant and interactive communities.

Key technologies and concepts underpinning Web 2.0 include the rise of JavaScript, which allowed for dynamic updates on web pages without the need for complete reloads. This enabled the development of more interactive interfaces, such as drag-and-drop functionality and real-time data updates. AJAX (Asynchronous JavaScript and XML) emerged as a powerful technique, enabling web applications to retrieve data from servers in the background, further enhancing the user experience.

Web 2.0 also introduced the concept of user-generated content, where individuals could create and share their own content, such as blog posts, videos, and photos. Platforms like YouTube, Flickr, and WordPress enabled users to express themselves and build online communities around shared interests. Social networking sites like Facebook and Twitter gained immense popularity, revolutionizing how people connect and communicate.

Section 3: The Need for Web 3.0

While Web 2.0 brought about significant advancements in user participation and content creation, it also exposed certain limitations. Issues such as data privacy, information overload, and lack of interoperability became apparent as the web continued to grow exponentially.

Web 3.0, often referred to as the Semantic Web or the Intelligent Web, aims to address these limitations by focusing on the seamless integration of data, artificial intelligence, and decentralized architectures. It envisions a web where information is structured, linked, and understood by machines, enabling more intelligent and personalized user experiences.

Web 3.0 seeks to utilize emerging technologies such as machine learning, natural language processing, and blockchain to create a more interconnected and secure web ecosystem. It emphasizes the use of standardized data formats, such as the Resource Description Framework (RDF) and linked data principles, to enable the sharing and integration of information across diverse platforms and applications.

The advent of Web 3.0 holds the potential for smarter search engines that can provide highly relevant and context-aware results, personalized recommendations, and intelligent virtual assistants that can understand and respond to natural language queries. It also aims to empower individuals by giving them greater control over their data, allowing for more transparent and secure interactions.

As the web continues to evolve, the transition from Web 1.0 to Web 2.0 and the ongoing development of Web 3.0 demonstrate the ever-changing nature of the digital landscape. Each phase builds upon its predecessor, pushing the boundaries of what is possible and driving innovation to create a more inclusive, intelligent, and connected web.

Chapter 2:
Understanding Web 3.0

Section 1: Defining Web 3.0: Characteristics and Principles

Web 3.0, also known as the Semantic Web or the Intelligent Web, represents the next phase in the evolution of the World Wide Web. It aims to create a more intelligent, interconnected, and decentralized web ecosystem. Web 3.0 is characterized by several key principles and characteristics that set it apart from its predecessors.

1. Structured and Linked Data: Web 3.0 emphasizes the use of standardized data formats, such as RDF (Resource Description Framework), to structure and link information on the web. This allows for more meaningful connections between data points, enabling machines to understand and process information more effectively.

2. Contextual and Personalized Experiences: Web 3.0 aims to deliver more contextually relevant and personalized experiences to users. By leveraging machine learning and natural language processing techniques, the web can understand user preferences, behavior, and intent, providing tailored recommendations, search results, and interactive interfaces.

3. Interoperability and Integration: Web 3.0 seeks to overcome the problem of data silos by promoting interoperability and data integration across different platforms, applications, and services. Linked data principles facilitate the seamless exchange and combination of information, enabling more comprehensive and interconnected knowledge networks.

Section 2: The Role of Blockchain Technology

One of the fundamental technologies underpinning Web 3.0 is blockchain. A blockchain is a decentralized and immutable ledger that records transactions across a network of computers. It offers several key features that align with the principles of Web 3.0.

1. Decentralization: Blockchain technology enables decentralized architectures by eliminating the need for a central authority or intermediary. Instead, data and transactions are distributed across a network of nodes, ensuring transparency, resilience, and censorship resistance.
2. Trust and Transparency: Blockchain introduces a trust layer by providing a tamper-resistant and auditable record of transactions. The transparent nature of the blockchain allows participants to verify the integrity and history of data, enhancing trust in the system.
3. Smart Contracts: Web 3.0 leverages smart contracts, which are self-executing contracts with predefined rules and conditions encoded on the blockchain. Smart contracts enable automated and secure interactions, eliminating the need for intermediaries and reducing the risk of fraud or manipulation.

Section 3: Decentralization and Distributed Consensus

Web 3.0 embraces the concept of decentralization, aiming to distribute power, control, and decision-making across the network. In Web 3.0, consensus mechanisms, such as Proof-of-Work (PoW) and Proof-of-Stake (PoS), are utilized to enable agreement and coordination among network participants.

1. Consensus Algorithms: Consensus algorithms ensure that all nodes in a decentralized network agree on the validity and order of transactions. These algorithms facilitate trust and prevent malicious activities, enabling secure and reliable interactions.
2. Distributed Applications (dApps): Web 3.0 fosters the development of dApps, which are applications that run on decentralized networks and utilize smart contracts for their operation. These applications leverage the collective computing power and storage capacity of network participants, promoting greater resilience, scalability, and censorship resistance.

Section 4: Trust, Security, and Privacy in Web 3.0

Web 3.0 places a strong emphasis on trust, security, and privacy, recognizing the need for individuals to have control over their data and ensuring secure interactions in a decentralized environment.

1. User Sovereignty: Web 3.0 promotes user sovereignty, allowing individuals to have ownership and control over their personal data. Through self-sovereign identity frameworks and decentralized authentication mechanisms, users can manage their digital identities and selectively disclose information as needed.
2. Encryption and Security: Web 3.0 employs robust encryption techniques to protect data privacy and secure communication channels. Cryptographic protocols and decentralized key management systems help prevent unauthorized access and ensure data integrity.
3. Auditability and Transparency: The transparent nature of blockchain technology enables greater auditability and accountability. Public blockchains allow anyone to verify the

accuracy and integrity of transactions, promoting transparency in the web ecosystem.

Web 3.0 seeks to address the shortcomings of previous web iterations by leveraging technologies such as blockchain, decentralization, and advanced data processing techniques. By combining these elements, Web 3.0 aims to create a more intelligent, trustworthy, and user-centric web experience.

Chapter 3:
Building Blocks of Web 3.0

Section 1: Decentralized Networks and Protocols

One of the foundational building blocks of Web 3.0 is the utilization of decentralized networks and protocols. Decentralization promotes resilience, censorship resistance, and the removal of single points of failure. Several technologies and concepts enable the establishment of decentralized networks in Web 3.0:

1. Peer-to-Peer (P2P) Networks: P2P networks facilitate direct communication and resource sharing between participants, eliminating the need for intermediaries. By leveraging distributed architectures, P2P networks enhance scalability, fault tolerance, and user autonomy.

2. Distributed Ledger Technology (DLT): DLT, such as blockchain and directed acyclic graph (DAG) technologies, form the basis of decentralized networks in Web 3.0. These distributed ledgers enable transparent, secure, and immutable record-keeping, ensuring trust and enabling decentralized consensus.

3. InterPlanetary File System (IPFS): IPFS is a protocol that allows the decentralized storage and retrieval of files across a distributed network. IPFS utilizes content-based addressing and peer-to-peer

connectivity, making data resilient, accessible, and censorship-resistant.

Section 2: Smart Contracts: Enabling Programmable Transactions

Smart contracts play a pivotal role in Web 3.0 by enabling programmable and self-executing agreements on decentralized platforms. Built on blockchain technology, smart contracts automatically enforce predefined rules and conditions, eliminating the need for intermediaries and enhancing trust. Key aspects of smart contracts include:

1. Code-Based Contracts: Smart contracts replace traditional legal agreements with programmable code, executing actions automatically when specific conditions are met. This automation reduces the risk of manipulation and allows for transparent and efficient transactional processes.
2. Immutable and Verifiable Execution: Smart contracts are executed on the blockchain, providing immutability and verifiability. Once deployed, smart contracts cannot be modified, ensuring trust in the execution and outcome of transactions.
3. Decentralized Applications (dApps): dApps leverage smart contracts as the underlying infrastructure for their operation. These decentralized applications interact with smart contracts on the blockchain, offering a wide range of functionalities, such as financial services, decentralized exchanges, and governance mechanisms.

Section 3: Tokenization and Digital Assets

Tokenization is a fundamental concept in Web 3.0, representing the transformation of real-world or digital assets into tokens on a blockchain. These tokens can represent ownership, access rights, or other forms of value. Key aspects of tokenization and digital assets include:

1. Utility Tokens: Utility tokens enable access to specific products, services, or functionalities within a decentralized ecosystem. They serve as a medium of exchange or a unit of value within a specific dApp or network.
2. Security Tokens: Security tokens represent ownership in an underlying asset, such as equity in a company or shares in a real estate property. Security tokens comply with regulatory frameworks and offer fractional ownership and liquidity to investors.
3. Non-Fungible Tokens (NFTs): NFTs represent unique and indivisible digital assets, such as artwork, collectibles, or virtual real estate. NFTs enable provenance, authenticity, and scarcity in the digital realm, revolutionizing the concept of ownership and digital rights.

Section 4: Interoperability and Data Portability

Interoperability and data portability are essential for Web 3.0 to create a seamless and connected web experience. By enabling interoperability between different protocols and platforms, data can flow freely, leading to enhanced user experiences and innovation. Key considerations in interoperability and data portability include:

1. Standardization and Open Protocols: Web 3.0 emphasizes the use of open protocols and standards, enabling different platforms and applications to communicate and share data seamlessly. Open protocols foster collaboration, interoperability, and prevent vendor lock-in.
2. Cross-Chain and Cross-Protocol Communication: Interoperability solutions, such as blockchain bridges and cross-chain communication protocols, facilitate the transfer of assets and data across different blockchain networks. These solutions enable the exchange of value and information between otherwise siloed ecosystems.

Section 5: Identity Management in Web 3.0

Web 3.0 introduces innovative approaches to identity management, empowering individuals with control over their digital identities and personal data. Key considerations in identity management within Web 3.0 include:

1. Self-Sovereign Identity (SSI): SSI enables individuals to have ownership and control over their digital identities. It allows users to manage and selectively disclose their personal data without relying on centralized identity providers.
2. Decentralized Identity (DID): DIDs are unique identifiers anchored on a blockchain or distributed ledger. DIDs provide a secure and verifiable way to authenticate and establish trust in digital interactions without disclosing unnecessary personal information.
3. Identity Providers and Verification: Web 3.0 incorporates decentralized identity providers and verification mechanisms. These solutions enable users to prove their identity and reputation through cryptographic proofs, reducing reliance on centralized authorities.

In Web 3.0, these building blocks work together to create a more decentralized, programmable, and user-centric web experience. The utilization of decentralized networks, smart contracts, tokenization, interoperability, and identity management fosters innovation, trust, and inclusion in the evolving web ecosystem.

Chapter 4:
Web 3.0 Applications and Use Cases

Section 1: Decentralized Finance (DeFi)

Decentralized Finance, or DeFi, represents one of the most prominent and transformative applications of Web 3.0. DeFi leverages blockchain technology and smart contracts to create an open and permissionless financial ecosystem. Key aspects of DeFi include:

1. Decentralized Exchanges: Web 3.0 enables the development of decentralized exchanges (DEXs), where users can trade cryptocurrencies directly, eliminating the need for intermediaries. DEXs provide enhanced security, transparency, and liquidity while enabling peer-to-peer transactions.
2. Decentralized Lending and Borrowing: Web 3.0 facilitates decentralized lending and borrowing platforms, allowing individuals to lend their assets and earn interest, or borrow assets against collateral. These platforms operate autonomously through smart contracts, providing efficient and transparent financial services.
3. Stablecoins and Decentralized Stablecoin Protocols: Stablecoins are cryptocurrencies designed to maintain a stable value, often pegged to a fiat currency. Web 3.0 introduces decentralized

stablecoin protocols, enabling users to hold and transact with stable digital assets, providing stability and avoiding volatility.

Section 2: Supply Chain Management and Traceability

Web 3.0 offers transformative solutions for supply chain management and traceability, enhancing transparency, accountability, and efficiency in complex global supply chains. Key aspects of supply chain management and traceability in Web 3.0 include:

1. Immutable and Transparent Records: Utilizing blockchain technology, Web 3.0 enables the creation of immutable and transparent records of supply chain transactions. This enhances visibility and traceability, reducing fraud, counterfeiting, and improving accountability.
2. Provenance and Authenticity Verification: Web 3.0 enables the tracking of products throughout the supply chain, allowing consumers to verify the origin, authenticity, and quality of goods. This enhances trust and enables consumers to make more informed purchasing decisions.
3. Supply Chain Automation and Optimization: Web 3.0 facilitates the integration of IoT devices, smart sensors, and automation technologies into supply chain management. This enables real-time monitoring, automated data collection, and optimization of supply chain processes, leading to improved efficiency and cost savings.

Section 3: Decentralized Social Media and Content Platforms

Web 3.0 brings significant advancements to social media and content platforms, addressing issues related to centralized control, data privacy, and censorship. Key aspects of decentralized social media and content platforms include:

1. User Ownership and Control: Web 3.0 platforms empower users by giving them ownership and control over their data, eliminating the dominance of centralized platforms. Users can choose to monetize their content, have transparent rules, and participate in governance decisions.
2. Censorship Resistance: Decentralized social media platforms leverage blockchain technology to create censorship-resistant environments. Content cannot be easily removed or manipulated, ensuring freedom of expression and combating the spread of misinformation.
3. Content Monetization: Web 3.0 platforms introduce innovative monetization models, such as micro-payments, token rewards, and decentralized advertising. Content creators can directly monetize their work, bypassing intermediaries and receiving fair compensation for their contributions.

Section 4: Internet of Things (IoT) and Web 3.0

Web 3.0 and the Internet of Things (IoT) converge to create a more connected and intelligent ecosystem. Web 3.0 augments IoT applications with decentralized protocols, enhanced security, and interoperability. Key aspects of IoT and Web 3.0 include:

1. Secure Data Exchange: Web 3.0 enables secure and peer-to-peer data exchange between IoT devices using blockchain technology. Smart contracts and decentralized protocols ensure trust and enable secure communication and data sharing.
2. Trusted Identity and Access Management: Web 3.0 introduces decentralized identity management for IoT devices, enabling secure authentication, access control, and data ownership. This ensures the integrity and confidentiality of IoT data and promotes interoperability between different IoT networks.
3. Autonomous Device Coordination: Web 3.0 facilitates the coordination and cooperation of autonomous IoT devices

through decentralized consensus mechanisms. Devices can autonomously reach agreements, execute transactions, and perform tasks without relying on centralized intermediaries.

Section 5: Healthcare and Personal Data Ownership

Web 3.0 introduces transformative possibilities for healthcare by empowering individuals with ownership and control over their personal health data. Key aspects of healthcare and personal data ownership in Web 3.0 include:

1. Personal Health Records (PHRs): Web 3.0 enables individuals to manage their PHRs securely on decentralized platforms. Individuals have control over who can access their data, facilitating improved privacy, interoperability, and personalized healthcare.
2. Data Monetization and Research: Web 3.0 allows individuals to choose to share their health data securely and selectively with healthcare providers, researchers, and pharmaceutical companies. Users can be incentivized through tokenized rewards for contributing to medical research and advancements.
3. Medical Supply Chain and Drug Traceability: Web 3.0 ensures transparency and traceability in the medical supply chain, reducing counterfeit drugs, improving drug safety, and enhancing patient trust. Immutable records and smart contracts enable the verification of drug authenticity and the tracking of supply chain processes.

Web 3.0 applications and use cases span various industries, transforming traditional practices and introducing novel approaches to finance, supply chain management, social media, IoT, healthcare, and personal data ownership. As Web 3.0 continues to evolve, its potential for innovation and disruption in these domains is vast and promising.

Chapter 5:
Web 3.0 and Industries

Section 1: Banking and Finance

Web 3.0 brings transformative changes to the banking and finance industry, disrupting traditional financial systems and introducing innovative solutions. Key aspects of Web 3.0 in banking and finance include:

1. Decentralized Financial Infrastructure: Web 3.0 enables the development of decentralized financial infrastructure, offering financial services without relying on intermediaries. Decentralized finance (DeFi) platforms allow individuals to lend, borrow, trade, and invest in a peer-to-peer manner, promoting financial inclusivity and reducing costs.

2. Programmable Money and Smart Contracts: Web 3.0 introduces programmable money through cryptocurrencies and smart contracts. Smart contracts automate financial agreements, enforce predefined conditions, and enable complex financial instruments such as decentralized lending, decentralized exchanges, and prediction markets.

3. Cross-Border Payments and Remittances: Web 3.0 facilitates faster, cheaper, and more efficient cross-border payments and remittances. By leveraging cryptocurrencies and blockchain

technology, individuals can send and receive funds globally with reduced fees, faster settlement times, and increased transparency.

Section 2: Healthcare and Medical Research

Web 3.0 revolutionizes the healthcare and medical research industry, enabling greater accessibility, interoperability, and privacy of health data. Key aspects of Web 3.0 in healthcare and medical research include:

1. Personal Health Data Ownership: Web 3.0 empowers individuals with ownership and control over their personal health data. Decentralized platforms allow users to securely manage and selectively share their health information with healthcare providers, researchers, and institutions, enhancing privacy and interoperability.
2. Medical Research and Data Sharing: Web 3.0 facilitates the secure sharing and collaboration of medical research data. Blockchain technology ensures data integrity, provenance, and incentivizes data contributors through tokenized rewards, accelerating medical advancements and research breakthroughs.
3. Telemedicine and Remote Patient Monitoring: Web 3.0 enhances telemedicine and remote patient monitoring through secure and decentralized communication channels. Smart contracts enable automated payments, appointment scheduling, and secure data exchange between patients and healthcare providers.

Section 3: Education and E-Learning

Web 3.0 transforms the education and e-learning landscape, revolutionizing how knowledge is accessed, shared, and validated. Key aspects of Web 3.0 in education and e-learning include:

1. Decentralized Learning Platforms: Web 3.0 enables the development of decentralized learning platforms, where

educational content is stored on distributed networks. These platforms provide access to a wide range of educational resources, foster peer-to-peer interactions, and allow for decentralized credentialing.

2. Verified Credentials and Digital Certificates: Web 3.0 introduces verifiable credentials and digital certificates using decentralized identity systems. These credentials provide a secure and tamper-proof way to verify educational achievements, skills, and qualifications, enhancing trust and reducing fraud in the job market.

3. Peer-to-Peer Knowledge Sharing and Collaboration: Web 3.0 facilitates peer-to-peer knowledge sharing and collaboration, enabling learners to connect, interact, and collaborate directly with experts and peers globally. Smart contracts can be used to incentivize contributions, fostering a vibrant and engaged learning community.

Section 4: Energy and Sustainability

Web 3.0 plays a significant role in promoting energy efficiency, sustainability, and the transition to renewable energy sources. Key aspects of Web 3.0 in the energy and sustainability industry include:

1. Peer-to-Peer Energy Trading: Web 3.0 enables peer-to-peer energy trading through decentralized energy platforms. Blockchain technology and smart contracts facilitate transparent, secure, and automated energy transactions between producers and consumers, promoting energy independence and grid resiliency.

2. Energy Data Management and Optimization: Web 3.0 allows for the secure collection, sharing, and analysis of energy data. Distributed ledger technology ensures data integrity, and artificial intelligence algorithms optimize energy consumption, enabling better energy management and efficiency.

3. Renewable Energy Certificate (REC) Tracking: Web 3.0 facilitates the tracking and verification of Renewable Energy Certificates (RECs). Blockchain-based systems provide transparent and auditable records of renewable energy generation, supporting carbon accounting and sustainable energy practices.

Section 5: Government and Governance

Web 3.0 introduces new possibilities for transparent, inclusive, and decentralized governance models. Key aspects of Web 3.0 in government and governance include:

1. Transparent and Trustworthy Elections: Web 3.0 enables the implementation of secure and transparent election systems. Blockchain-based voting platforms can enhance the integrity of the electoral process, ensuring accurate vote counting, tamper-proof records, and increased voter trust.
2. Immutable and Verifiable Government Records: Web 3.0 allows for the creation of immutable and verifiable government records. Distributed ledger technology ensures the integrity and transparency of public records, reducing the risk of corruption and enabling efficient access to government services.
3. Citizen Participation and Collaboration: Web 3.0 platforms promote citizen participation and collaboration in the decision-making process. Through decentralized governance mechanisms and token-based voting systems, citizens can actively contribute to policy-making, budget allocation, and community initiatives.

Web 3.0 has the potential to revolutionize various industries, including banking and finance, healthcare and medical research, education and e-learning, energy and sustainability, and government and governance. As these industries embrace the principles of decentralization, transparency, and user empowerment, the possibilities for innovation and positive impact continue to expand.

Chapter 6:
Web 3.0 Challenges and Solutions

Section 1: Scalability and Performance

One of the primary challenges of Web 3.0 is scalability and performance. As the adoption of decentralized applications and blockchain networks grows, the infrastructure must be able to handle increased transaction volumes and data processing. Key challenges and solutions include:

1. Scalability: Blockchain networks face scalability issues due to their consensus mechanisms and decentralized nature. Solutions such as sharding, layer-2 protocols (e.g., Lightning Network), and off-chain solutions aim to increase transaction throughput and network capacity.

2. Performance: Web 3.0 applications need to provide responsive and seamless user experiences. Optimizations like improving transaction confirmation times, reducing latency, and enhancing network efficiency are crucial for enhancing performance.

Section 2: User Experience and Adoption

User experience and adoption are critical factors for the success of Web 3.0. Overcoming the complexity and technical barriers associated with decentralized applications is essential. Key challenges and solutions include:

1. User-Friendly Interfaces: Web 3.0 applications need intuitive interfaces that abstract the underlying complexities of blockchain technology. User-friendly wallets, dApps, and decentralized browsers are essential for attracting mainstream users.
2. Education and Awareness: Educating users about the benefits and functionalities of Web 3.0 is crucial for adoption. Efforts to raise awareness through educational resources, tutorials, and community engagement can bridge the knowledge gap.

Section 3: Regulatory and Legal Considerations

Web 3.0 introduces regulatory and legal considerations that need to be addressed for widespread adoption and compliance. Key challenges and solutions include:

1. Regulatory Clarity: Existing regulations often lag behind the pace of technological innovation, leading to uncertainty. Governments and regulatory bodies need to provide clear guidelines and frameworks to foster innovation while addressing concerns related to privacy, consumer protection, and financial regulations.
2. Compliance and Identity Verification: Web 3.0 applications require robust identity verification and compliance mechanisms to prevent fraud, money laundering, and illicit activities. Compliance solutions that balance privacy and security are necessary to meet regulatory requirements.

Section 4: Interoperability Challenges

Interoperability is vital for the seamless integration of various Web 3.0 platforms and blockchain networks. Key challenges and solutions include:

1. Standardization: Developing common standards and protocols allows different blockchain networks to communicate and share data effectively. Standardization efforts across blockchain platforms facilitate interoperability and promote collaboration.
2. Cross-Chain Communication: Solutions such as blockchain bridges, interoperability protocols, and cross-chain atomic swaps enable the transfer of assets and data between different blockchain networks, enhancing interoperability.

Section 5: Overcoming Trust and Security Concerns

Trust and security are significant concerns in the Web 3.0 landscape. Building trust in decentralized systems and ensuring the security of user data are critical for adoption. Key challenges and solutions include:

1. Data Privacy and Confidentiality: Web 3.0 applications must prioritize data privacy, giving users control over their personal information. Implementing encryption, secure storage solutions, and decentralized identity systems can protect user data and enhance privacy.
2. Auditing and Code Review: Open-source code and smart contracts must undergo rigorous auditing and review processes to identify vulnerabilities and security flaws. Formal verification methods and third-party audits help ensure the integrity and security of Web 3.0 applications.

Web 3.0 presents various challenges that need to be addressed for its widespread adoption and success. Scalability, user experience, regulatory compliance, interoperability, trust, and security are among the key areas that require ongoing innovation, collaboration, and technological advancements. Overcoming these challenges will pave the way for a more decentralized, inclusive, and user-centric web ecosystem.

Chapter 7:
The Future of Web 3.0

Section 1: Emerging Trends and Technologies

The future of Web 3.0 holds exciting possibilities as emerging trends and technologies continue to shape its evolution. Key areas to watch include:

1. Internet of Things (IoT) Integration: The integration of Web 3.0 with IoT devices will enable secure and decentralized communication, data exchange, and autonomous device coordination, creating a more interconnected and intelligent network of devices.

2. Web 3.0 and Extended Reality (XR): Web 3.0 has the potential to enhance immersive experiences by integrating XR technologies such as virtual reality (VR) and augmented reality (AR). Decentralized content creation, ownership, and distribution will transform how we interact with digital environments.

3. Web 3.0 and Data Marketplaces: Decentralized data marketplaces will emerge, allowing individuals to securely sell and monetize their data. This shift towards user-centric data ownership and control will incentivize data sharing and drive innovation across industries.

Section 2: Web 3.0 and Artificial Intelligence

The convergence of Web 3.0 and artificial intelligence (AI) will lead to powerful synergies and advancements. Key developments include:

1. Decentralized AI: Web 3.0 enables decentralized AI models and training, preserving data privacy and security while fostering collaboration and knowledge sharing. Federated learning, where AI models are trained across multiple devices without centralizing data, will become more prevalent.
2. AI-Driven Personalization: Web 3.0 will leverage AI algorithms to deliver personalized experiences, recommendations, and services to users. Intelligent agents and chatbots powered by AI will enhance user interactions and simplify complex tasks.

Section 3: Potential Disruptions in Various Industries

Web 3.0 has the potential to disrupt various industries, reshaping business models and processes. Key industries to be impacted include:

1. Finance and Banking: Web 3.0's decentralized finance (DeFi) will challenge traditional banking models, enabling greater financial inclusivity, reduced intermediation, and new forms of value exchange.
2. Supply Chain and Logistics: Web 3.0's transparent and immutable records will revolutionize supply chain management, ensuring traceability, reducing fraud, and enhancing efficiency and sustainability.
3. Healthcare and Life Sciences: Web 3.0 will empower individuals with ownership and control over their health data, enabling personalized medicine, medical research advancements, and secure sharing of health information.

Section 4: Collaboration and Decentralized Ecosystems

Web 3.0 fosters collaboration and the emergence of decentralized ecosystems. Key aspects include:

1. Decentralized Governance: Web 3.0 will see the rise of decentralized governance models, where decision-making is distributed among stakeholders, promoting transparency, inclusivity, and community-driven development.
2. Collaborative Economy: Web 3.0 will facilitate peer-to-peer interactions and value exchange, empowering individuals to participate in collaborative economies. Decentralized marketplaces, sharing economies, and tokenized ecosystems will enable new economic models.

Section 5: User-Centric and Inclusive Web 3.0

The future of Web 3.0 will prioritize user-centricity and inclusivity, placing individuals at the center of their digital experiences. Key considerations include:

1. Personalized and Privacy-Enhancing Technologies: Web 3.0 will leverage advanced technologies to deliver personalized experiences while respecting user privacy and data ownership rights. Encryption, decentralized identity systems, and data minimization techniques will be prioritized.
2. Digital Sovereignty: Web 3.0 will empower individuals with digital sovereignty, ensuring they have control over their data, digital identities, and online presence. Users will have the ability to manage and monetize their digital assets and online activities.

Web 3.0 represents the next phase of the internet's evolution, promising greater decentralization, user empowerment, and technological advancements. By embracing emerging trends, fostering collaboration, disrupting industries, and prioritizing user-centricity, the future of Web 3.0 holds immense potential to reshape how we interact with the digital world and drive positive social and economic change.

Chapter 8:
Web 3.0 and Society

Section 1: Democratization of Information and Power

Web 3.0 brings about the democratization of information and power, shifting the dynamics of society. Key aspects include:

1. Access to Information: Web 3.0 provides equal access to information, eliminating traditional gatekeepers and enabling individuals to access knowledge and resources globally. Open access to information promotes education, empowers individuals, and fosters innovation.
2. Decentralized Decision-Making: Web 3.0's decentralized governance models allow for collective decision-making, giving individuals and communities a voice in shaping policies, initiatives, and systems. This redistribution of power promotes inclusivity, transparency, and accountability.

Section 2: Empowering Individuals and Communities

Web 3.0 empowers individuals and communities by granting them greater control, ownership, and participation in the digital realm. Key aspects include:

1. Digital Identity and Ownership: Web 3.0 enables individuals to have self-sovereign digital identities, ensuring control over their personal data and online presence. This empowerment fosters trust, privacy, and autonomy.
2. Collaborative Communities: Web 3.0 facilitates the formation of collaborative communities that leverage decentralized networks to exchange ideas, resources, and value. Individuals can connect, contribute, and create together, fostering a sense of belonging and shared purpose.

Section 3: Ethical Considerations and Societal Impact

Web 3.0 raises important ethical considerations and has a profound impact on society. Key aspects include:

1. Data Privacy and Security: Web 3.0 calls for robust privacy and security measures to protect individuals' data and prevent unauthorized access. Ethical considerations should prioritize data protection and informed consent.
2. Transparency and Accountability: Web 3.0 encourages transparency and accountability across various sectors. Smart contracts and blockchain technology can ensure auditability, reducing corruption and promoting trust.

Section 4: Bridging the Digital Divide

Web 3.0 has the potential to bridge the digital divide, ensuring equal opportunities for all individuals. Key aspects include:

1. Access to Infrastructure: Web 3.0 aims to provide infrastructure and connectivity to underserved regions, narrowing the digital divide. Decentralized networks and low-cost technologies can facilitate internet access, enabling economic and educational opportunities.

2. Financial Inclusion: Web 3.0's decentralized finance (DeFi) can empower the unbanked and underbanked populations by providing access to financial services and enabling peer-to-peer transactions. This inclusion can contribute to economic growth and poverty reduction.

Section 5: Web 3.0 as a Catalyst for Social Change

Web 3.0 serves as a catalyst for social change, empowering individuals and driving positive transformations. Key aspects include:

1. Decentralized Philanthropy and Impact Investing: Web 3.0 enables decentralized philanthropy through crowdfunding platforms and impact investing. These mechanisms promote social initiatives, sustainable development, and support for marginalized communities.
2. Civic Engagement and Activism: Web 3.0 empowers individuals to engage in civic activities and grassroots movements, facilitating collective action and social activism. Decentralized platforms provide spaces for collaboration, coordination, and advocacy.

Web 3.0's impact on society extends beyond technological advancements. It reshapes power structures, promotes individual empowerment, fosters ethical considerations, bridges divides, and acts as a catalyst for social change. Embracing the potential of Web 3.0 can lead to a more inclusive, equitable, and participatory society.

Chapter 9:
Investing and Entrepreneurship in Web 3.0

Section 1: Investment Opportunities in Web 3.0

Web 3.0 presents a wide range of investment opportunities for individuals and institutions. Key aspects include:

1. Decentralized Finance (DeFi): Investment opportunities arise in decentralized finance protocols, lending platforms, liquidity provision, yield farming, and governance tokens. DeFi offers potential returns and diversification options within the cryptocurrency ecosystem.

2. Digital Assets and NFTs: Non-Fungible Tokens (NFTs) provide investment opportunities in the digital art, collectibles, gaming, and virtual real estate sectors. Digital assets offer unique value propositions and the potential for value appreciation.

Section 2: Startup Ecosystem and Funding Landscape

The startup ecosystem and funding landscape in Web 3.0 are evolving rapidly, providing opportunities for entrepreneurs and investors. Key aspects include:

1. Incubators and Accelerators: Web 3.0-focused incubators and accelerators support early-stage startups by providing mentorship, resources, and networking opportunities. These programs help entrepreneurs refine their ideas and gain traction in the market.
2. Initial Coin Offerings (ICOs) and Token Sales: ICOs and token sales have been popular fundraising mechanisms in Web 3.0. They allow startups to raise capital by selling tokens or digital assets, providing investors with early access to projects and potential returns.

Section 3: Navigating the Web 3.0 Business Landscape

Navigating the Web 3.0 business landscape requires an understanding of the unique challenges and opportunities it presents. Key aspects include:

1. Regulatory Compliance: Startups need to navigate the evolving regulatory landscape associated with cryptocurrencies, token offerings, and decentralized applications. Compliance with legal requirements ensures legitimacy and builds trust with investors and users.
2. Market and Competitive Analysis: Entrepreneurs must conduct thorough market and competitive analysis to identify gaps, differentiate their offerings, and address user needs. Understanding the target audience and competitors is crucial for sustainable growth.

Section 4: Skills and Resources for Web 3.0 Entrepreneurs

Web 3.0 entrepreneurship requires a specific skill set and access to relevant resources. Key aspects include:

1. Technical Proficiency: Web 3.0 entrepreneurs benefit from a strong understanding of blockchain technology, smart contracts, decentralized networks, and cryptography. Technical proficiency enables the development and management of innovative solutions.

2. Community Engagement and Networking: Active participation in Web 3.0 communities, attending conferences, and building networks are vital for entrepreneurs. Engaging with like-minded individuals and industry experts fosters collaboration, learning, and potential partnerships.

3. Continuous Learning and Adaptability: Web 3.0 is a rapidly evolving space, and entrepreneurs need to stay updated with the latest trends, technologies, and industry developments. Continuous learning, adaptability, and agility are key attributes for success.

Investing and entrepreneurship in Web 3.0 offer exciting opportunities to be at the forefront of technological innovation. Understanding the investment landscape, accessing funding, navigating the business environment, and acquiring the necessary skills and resources are essential for entrepreneurs and investors to thrive in this dynamic ecosystem.

Thank you for purchasing this book!

For additional reading on Blockchain Technology and Digital Currencies, please check-out my other book:

1. Cryptocurrency Chronicles
   Unlocking The Secrets Of Blockchain Technology

2. A Deep Dive Into The Top 50 Cryptocurrencies
   A DYOR (Do Your Own Research) Guide

3. Common Crypto Investment Pitfalls and How To Avoid
   A DYOR (Do Your Own Research) Guide

4. The Digital Revolution
   Central Bank Digital Currencies (CBDC) Unveiled